Elephant Tricks

words by Amanda Graham
illustrated by Neil Curtis

"Look at me," said the first elephant. "I can do a clever trick. I can juggle some apples."

"Look at me," said the next elephant. "I can do a clever trick, too. I can stack bananas."

"Look at me," said the next elephant.
"I can do a clever trick, too. I can
balance on my trunk."

"Look at me," said the next elephant. "I can do a clever trick, too. I can walk on stilts."

"Look at me," said the next elephant. "I can do a clever trick, too. I can lift a heavy log."

"Look at me," said the last elephant. "I can do a clever trick, too. I can swing on a rope."

"Uh oh," said the other elephants.

Whoosh! Crash!

The elephants spun.

The elephants tumbled.

"Look at us!" said the last elephant.

"We can do a clever trick."

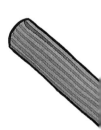

15

"We can make a tower."